If UFO's Are Real

By Larry Koss,
Editorial Director

Published By
Capstone Press, Inc.
Mankato, Minnesota USA

Distri'

◁P CHILDR
CH

D1261275

CIP
LIBRARY OF CONGRESS CATALOGING IN PUBLICATION DATA

If UFOS are real / Larry Koss, project editor.
    p. cm.
Summary: Examines sightings, studies, and projects related to unidentified flying objects and discusses the search for life in space.

ISBN 1-56065-094-X:
1. Unidentified flying objects--Juvenile literature.
2. Unidentified flying objects--Research--Juvenile literature.
[1. Unidentified flying objects.] I. Koss, Larry.
TL789.I36   1991
001.9'42--dc20   91-19908
                                          CIP
                                          AC

PHOTO CREDITS

U.S. Navy: 4
Antonia Humeeus: 7, 18, 25, 31, 40, 43

CAPSTONE PRESS
Box 669, Mankato, MN 56001

Contents

INTRODUCTION
By John Schuessler

We live in exciting times. Airplanes fly to the farthest parts of the globe. Space shuttle flights are common. We have landed on the moon and driven its surface in a moon buggy. The Voyager Space Probe has passed Neptune and is headed out toward the stars. Scientists are searching for signs of life in outer space, and they expect to find them.

We have always been curious about the sky. We have always wanted to know "is there anyone else out there?"

Closer to the planet earth, unidentified flying objects have been seen. We call them "UFOs" for short. Many people have seen them. A Gallup Poll found that more than 15,000,000 Americans have seen UFOs. There have also been sightings in Europe, South America, Australia and other places.

Some people believe all UFOs are simple things that can be explained. Other people say that UFOs are a real mystery. How can we tell which is true? We can ask the people who study UFOs. We can ask for facts as well as opinions. More and more educated people know about UFOs, including many scientists and engineers who are studying them.

It is no surprise that many pilots have seen UFOs. Pilots are trained to be good observers. They must quickly spot and identify anything in the sky near them.

Engineers and astronauts have seen UFOs, too. They have also been trained to note carefully what they have seen.

Each day there are new discoveries about science, space travel, and the search for life in space. There is a lot to learn, so it is important to keep an open mind. That means being ready for new ideas. It means not saying "That is impossible!" before knowing all the facts. This book will tell you about the excitement felt by people who want to learn about new ideas. They view the future as a time to grow, and to help mankind.

They are always asking questions. You may want to join them as they search for answers.

One such person is Dr. Richard Haines. Dr. Haines is a former NASA research scientist and maintains a computerized collection of over 3,000 UFO sightings reported by pilots.

Two unexplained bodies flying horizontally over the Zurich, Switzerland Airport in the summer of 1966.

PILOTS SEE AND REPORT UFOS
By Richard F. Haines

Pilots have seen and reported UFOs for more than 50 years. There are more than 3000 cases of UFO sightings from military, private, and airline pilots. Test pilots and astronauts have reported UFOs, too. Air crew sightings made from high altitudes often are very good UFO cases. There are several reasons why.

Pilots are usually well educated, stable men or women who have been trained to recognize different things in the sky. Their eyesight must be very keen. You may just barely see a plane in the distance, but a pilot will say, "Yes, that is a 747, and it belongs to United Airlines." He can recognize the shape of the plane, and he can even see enough of the way it is painted to know the rest. Pilots have learned about unusual weather conditions, too. They know about astronomical events like meteors, and they know about balloons, military planes, and planes with unusual shapes. They would see the colorful markings on it. And they would see the wings, tail, and other man-made details.

There are other reasons why pilot reports are worth studying. Suppose a pilot looks down and sees a UFO below him. The ground below the UFO will be the "background of the picture." Now, if the plane is flying 10,000 feet above the ground, we know that the UFO must be less than 10,000 feet away. Knowing how big the UFO *looks* against the background, which is a known distance away, will help us find out how big the UFO really is.

It is always useful to see a UFO against some kind of background (ground, mountains, trees, clouds). Then we can tell what is the farthest away it could be. Maybe we can also tell something about its size. If you ever have a chance to take a picture of a UFO, try to get some background in the picture, too.

The chance that a UFO is a kite, balloon, or bird is less when the UFO is seen at a very high altitude. Of course a kite could have snapped its string and be floating free. But balloons would burst because of the thinner air pressure and birds do not fly at 30,000 feet.

Most pilots are professional people who value a good reputation. They do not want to risk losing their job by reporting something unless they are sure it was unusual. Most pilot reports are based on an actual sighting of something really strange.

Between 1942 and 1952, there were 283 UFO reports from pilots. Most of them were from American military pilots. Between 1973 and 1978, 60 percent of all pilot reports were made by foreign pilots and 40 percent by American pilots. That may mean that foreign airlines permitted their pilots to talk more about their sightings. Or, it may mean that there really were more sightings in places outside the United States where most foreign pilots fly.

How long do these sightings usually last? The average time the UFO was in view was over 7 minutes. One case in 1949 lasted 84 minutes. That's almost an hour and a half.

There seem to be about two dozen good reports each year from around the world. For some reason, July usually has the most sightings. Most sightings occur after dark. There is a jump in sightings between 10 p.m. and midnight, and another jump between 2:00 and 3:00 a.m. That's interesting, because there are very few airplanes flying at that hour. Do UFOs *come out* when airplanes *go in?*

It is usually true that the larger the number of pilot witnesses to an event, the more accurate the report will be. Certainly pilots can be fooled by strange sights, but they are still more accurate observers than most people.

Today most planes have equipment which could react to a nearby UFO. There might be static on the radio, or an image on a radar screen. Sometimes the plane's compass might go out of order.

In past UFO sightings, plane to ground radio contact has been broken, or there have been strange noises on the radio. Airplane cabin lights have dimmed when the UFO was near. Airplane engines have not worked right. Autopilots have gone out of order. On military planes, some of the weapon systems have failed. Whatever UFOs are, they seem to be able to affect things that work by electricity or magnetism.

It would not be unusual for a pilot to report a UFO if he saw a military test plane, but it is not likely that it would be seen. In order to keep the testing secret, most military test planes are not flown where they can be seen by anyone, including other pilots.

Some photographs of UFOs have been taken from the air. One was taken by a Japanese pilot during World War II. Back then, UFOs were called "Foo fighters." They were also seen by American, British, German, and other military pilots.

Another UFO photo was taken by Dr. J. Allen Hynek, the famous astronomer who founded the Center for UFO Studies. Dr. Hynek was on board an airliner when he noticed a round disc-like object they were passing. He quickly snapped a picture which also shows some clouds below the plane. The object has not been explained.

Another case took place on a clear sunny day, July 4, 1981, at 4:45 p.m. The Captain and two other crew members were flying an L-1011 jet airliner with more than 200 passengers on board. They had just passed over the western shore of

Lake Michigan, headed for Detroit at 37,000 feet. They were flying at almost 500 miles per hour. Suddenly the Captain saw a round shiny metallic object nearing them from the left side. It was slightly higher than their plane.

The pilot pointed the disc out to his co-pilot, thinking at first it was another plane. As they watched the object, it passed by their left side. They saw it turn rapidly on its axis, showing its other side. Then it changed course and slowly climbed away from them. The UFO was not like any plane they had ever seen before. It looked like two hub caps placed rim to rim with six black circles spaced along its edge. One black circle was centered on the bottom. The top looked like polished metal with a shallow pointed cone in the center. They saw no engines, wings, markings or seams. It did not alter its smooth and powerful flight.

The pilot had flown many different kinds of planes over many years, but he had never before seen anything like this object. He thought it must have come from out of this world. There are many thousands of reports similar to his.

ENGINEERS AND SCIENTISTS STUDY UFOS

By John Schuessler

Professor Herman Oberth, a German rocket scientist, studied hundreds of UFO reports. He thought UFOs were flying machines. He explained that some UFOs are seen to fly as fast as 42,000 miles per hour and are tracked on radar. So far, no machine built on earth can travel that fast. For that reason, Oberth said UFOs cannot have been built by humans.

One mystery about UFOs is called the "E-M Effect." "E-M" stands for *Electro-Magnetic*. Many times a UFO comes close to a car and the car motor stops. The car lights go out and the radio goes off. After the UFO leaves, the car runs fine again. What causes that? Engineers studying UFOs think something aboard the UFO, perhaps the propulsion system, (the energy system that makes it "go") causes this effect. It could be that a magnetic field around the UFO causes the cars electrical systems to fail.

Another UFO mystery is the silence of UFOs. Most times, UFOs make no noise at all. They speed past high-powered jets and are seen on radar flying thousands of miles per hour. Yet there is no engine sound, and no sonic boom. UFOs have been reported in space by our astronauts. We know that in space there would be no sound, but why are UFOs silent near the ground, where there is air to carry the sound waves? How can UFOs fly so fast?

Dr. Harley Rutledge of Cape Girardeau, Missouri, is a college physics professor. Dr. Rutledge is known as an excellent scientist. In 1973 he was asked to head an important UFO investigation. His job was to find out what hundreds of people were seeing in the skies over the southeast part of Missouri.

Soon Dr. Rutledge had gathered a team of scientists to help him look for UFOs. Within a few days he had 35 to 40 other experts ready to join him in his work. They used telescopes, sound detectors, and a number of fine cameras to track the UFOs. They also had instruments called electromatic wave analyzers.

The team worked hard for seven months. More than 70 of the sightings they investigated could be explained. The team believed they proved that UFOs are real. At the end of the study, Dr. Rutledge said: "They are intelligently controlled. I won't back down from anyone on that."

Some Engineers in Houston, Texas wondered what the inside of a UFO would look like. They had been inside planes and spacecraft, but never a UFO.

"What would be different about a UFO?" They asked. "How can we find out?" Then they thought "Why not talk to someone who had been inside a UFO!"

Their first step was to form a project team. They called their group the Vehicle Internal Systems Investigative Team, or VISIT for short. Although no one on the team had ever seen a UFO, they really wanted to talk with the people who had.

Many people claim they have been picked up by UFO occupants. They say they were taken inside the UFO and given physical exams. Then they were set free again. These people are called abductees. In a way, they were kidnapped by the beings, and for most people, it was pretty scary. The VISIT engineers decided to talk to as many abductees as possible to see what they could learn about the inside of the UFO.

The study is not over yet, but some patterns are emerging. While all abductees do not agree, many say the inside of a UFO is a cool temperature. It is brightly lit, and quiet. What they describe seems to be some type of spacecraft.

We are also learning about the size of the alien beings. Their legs must be short because their chairs are small and close to the floor. Sometimes there are windows located about 3 1/2 feet above the floor. While this would be just right for a human seated on a chair, the chairs are not placed near the windows. An alien about 4 feet tall could see fine out of those windows. A taller adult human would not be able to see out.

Control panel placements show how far an alien can reach with its long thin arms. The sizes of the knobs and switches help us know the shape of their hands. Their hands are thin with long fingers.

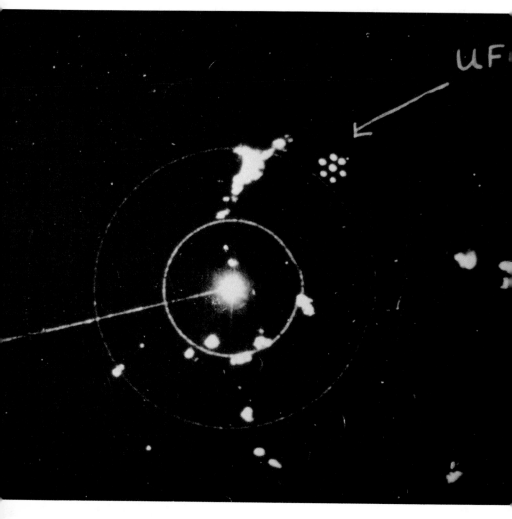

Seven "unidentified tracks" detected on the radar
of Washington's National Airport on the night of
July 20, 1952.

Engineers are excited about the results of the VISIT study. Yet they remind us that is only a study and not positive proof. One day we will have proof and then we will understand how UFOs fly higher and faster than our planes.

Understanding the inside of UFOs can help us learn how they fly. The VISIT engineers hope this knowledge will help their work in our own space program.

ASTRONOMERS AND UFOS
By John Schuessler

Dr. Clyde Tombaugh is a famous astronomer. He discovered the planet Pluto in 1930. "Discovering the ninth planet was an out-of-this-world thrill," he said. It happened after many months of hard work. Years later he saw a UFO with a long row of windows. He has been interested in UFOs ever since.

Dr. Frank Halstead was curator of the Darling Observatory in Duluth, Minnesota. He and his wife Ann were on a train, crossing the Mojave

Desert in California. They saw two shiny UFOs. The first one was shaped like a blimp. The second one was disc-shaped. Both objects flew along with the train for six or seven minutes. Then they began to rise and were soon out of sight. They went so fast it seemed like the train was standing still.

Dr. Peter Sturrock of Stanford University used an opinion poll to find out how astronomers felt about UFOs. A total of 1,356 astronomers answered. Eighty percent said they thought UFOs deserved scientific study. Sixty-two astronomers said they had seen UFOs.

One astronomer said he had seen a "classic flying saucer." It was solid and sharply outlined. As he neared the UFO, it went behind a cloud. His sighting was in the daytime.

Another astronomer said he saw a "silvery, disc-shaped object." It passed over the road, ahead of his car. Then it changed direction and shot up into the sky. Seconds later it looked like a star, hovering over a factory in the distance.

A number of UFOs were seen through telescopes. Some were detected on radar. One astronomer said he was an officer on a Navy ship when their radar picked up a UFO at 5,000 feet. The object stopped suddenly. Then it climbed straight up until it was out of range of the radar.

Two amateur astronomers had a close encounter with a UFO near St. Louis, Missouri. It was October 30, 1966. They were in the back yard watching for the Echo satellite. Suddenly a UFO passed right over their heads. They thought it was about 200 feet high. They said it was about 50 feet in diameter and looked like two soup bowls placed rim to rim. The whole object glowed like hot metal. Its color ranged from brown-orange to a light red-orange and its surface looked like the inside of a grapefruit. It was completely silent.

The world's leading authority on UFOs was Dr. J. Allen Hynek. For many years he was Professor of Astronomy at Northwestern University. Dr. Hynek made up the phrase "close encounters of the third kind." This phrase describes humans meeting aliens from space.

Dr. Hynek helped the U.S. Air Force for 20 years. His job was to study UFO reports to find the ones caused by meteors, planets, or other natural things. Dr. Hynek was a serious, thoughtful scientist. He said: "for a long time I thought we could just sweep all of this under the carpet and say it all had to be nonsense...But I have been driven to the other conclusion."

In 1973 Dr. Hynek opened the Center for UFO Studies in Evanston, Illinois. The Center was dedicated to the scientific investigation of UFOs. Dr. Hynek was careful in his work. He always looked for the facts and was open to new ideas. He helped bring scientific respectability to the study of UFOs.

ASTRONAUT SIGHTINGS
By John Schuessler

Many astronauts have reported seeing UFOs. Gordon Cooper, for example, reported a green object with a red tail as he flew on Mercury 8 in 1963.

Russian cosmonauts aboard Voskhod 2 reported a UFO just as they entered the earth's atmosphere. Three other Russian cosmonauts aboard Voskhod 1 said they were surrounded by a formation of fast-moving disc-shaped objects. Both sightings were in 1964.

UFOs were reported on at least five of the Gemini flights by our astronauts. Jim McDivitt said he photographed several objects. One was egg-shaped. It had an exhaust trail. Another was a large cylinder with "arms" sticking out. Some experts believe McDivitt saw the Russian Proton 3 spacecraft. Others are not so sure. Proton 3 was flying near the southern tip of South America. Gemini was near the coast of Africa. Could McDivitt have seen another craft hundreds of miles away?

NASA film experts have studied every picture taken by the astronauts. Some of the UFOs were found to be "space garbage" discarded by the crew. Other objects were satellites. NASA says it is satisfied that all the UFOs have been explained.

Some of the astronauts have talked about their feelings about UFOs and life in space. Jim McDivitt said "I really think that it is naive for us to think we're the only intelligent beings in the universe...when you think how big the universe really is. So, I think there are other intelligent beings someplace."

Astronaut Gene Cernan said: "I believe UFOs belong to someone else and they are from another civilization."

Gordon Cooper made a very strong statement at Cape Canaveral, Florida in 1973. He said "I believe UFOs, under intelligent control, have visited our planet for thousands of years."

Astronaut Deke Slayton said "You'd have to be very conceited to think a Supreme Being created this whole universe and we're the only ones with enough intelligence to go flying around."

Some people believe that UFOs followed the Apollo flights to the moon. Others say UFOs have been seen by Space Shuttle astronauts. Someday soon we will have humans permanently circling the earth in a space station. How will they deal with UFOs?

Taken by Jim McDivitt during Gemini 4 Mission on June 24, 1965.

NASA AND THE UFOS
By John Schessler

It is only natural to expect NASA to be interested in UFOs. NASA experts in science and engineering have made our space program possible. If UFOs are space vehicles, shouldn't NASA be interested in them?

President Carter thought so. He asked NASA to answer all the questions people asked about UFOs. But NASA did not want the job. In 1976 NASA said that UFOs flying in U.S. air space should be the responsibility of the Air Force. NASA's job is to manage a civilian space program. They also seek ways to use space technology back on earth.

In the space program, NASA scientists have been able to solve many tough problems. When something goes wrong, NASA brings the "hardware" into the lab for work. It's like bringing your car to the shop for service. The NASA experts usually know what to do. They nearly always solve the problem.

With UFOs it was a different story. NASA had nothing to bring into the laboratory. UFO reports and photos could not be tested by NASA. NASA needed to see the hardware. Without the evidence in their hands, NASA could not figure out how to investigate UFOs. They told President Carter they did not want to work on UFOs.

But NASA did agree to answer letters asking about UFOs. And if they were sent any real samples of UFO materials, the NASA laboratories would analyze them. Until that time, NASA only answers all UFO inquiries with a form letter. The letter says that there is no evidence that UFOs are a threat to the United States. It says there is no evidence that UFOs are any machines beyond known technology.

THE FRENCH UFO PROJECT
By John Schuessler

A group at the French space agency *does* study UFOs. The group is called GEPAN. It was formed in 1977. That was about the same time NASA told President Carter that they did not want to study UFOs.

Dr. Claude Pher was the first head of GEPAN, His group of experts included astronomers, physicists, doctors and engineers. He also asked the French police to help with the project. Whenever UFOs were reported, GEPAN would quickly send their experts to the scene.

The GEPAN team soon found out that UFO investigations were hard work. All UFOs could not be explained as something ordinary. They were not all in peoples' minds either. It was clear to GEPAN that something real was going on.

No one ever knows when or where UFOs will be seen. All the facts have to be gathered after something happens. The French scientists soon found that NASA was right about not being able to bring UFOs into the laboratory.

But GEPAN did not give up. They found ways to sort out the facts using computers to help them. Police reports helped the experts to arrive quickly at the scene. Then reports and samples could be collected while they were still fresh.

Here is a case which has not been explained, even after a thorough investigation by GEPAN:

A 55 year-old man, Renato Collini, saw a disc-shaped object fly over his head. He described the UFO as being like two bowls fastened together. Underneath, it had small landing pods.

Monsieur Collini could hear a strange whistling sound from the UFO. Soon it landed near a large pine tree. He moved closer. Standing on a hill he could see the UFO on the ground below him.

After a few minutes, the object started to whistle again. It rose off the ground in a cloud of dust. He was less than 100 feet from the UFO as it took off. He could easily see four openings on the bottom of the craft. There was no doubt in his mind that the object was real.

After the UFO was gone, Monsieur Collini walked to the spot where it had landed. He found a circle about 6 feet in diameter. There were also dents in the ground from the landing pods.

The GEPAN investigation was very thorough. Traces of the landing site were still visible 40 days later. Strangely, the grass and leaves under the UFO had been damaged. The chlorophyll was weakened. In the UFO landing site, young leaves looked old. There was only half the amount of chlorophyll that there should have been. Similar plant damage had happened in another UFO case in Minnesota.

The GEPAN scientists could not find out how the leaves had been hurt. It was not by nuclear radiation. Their best guess was that some type of electrical energy had caused the problem. This could be a clue to the propulsion system of the UFO. The French scientists could not solve the case of Monsieur Collini's UFO. They said "a very significant event" had happened on his farm.

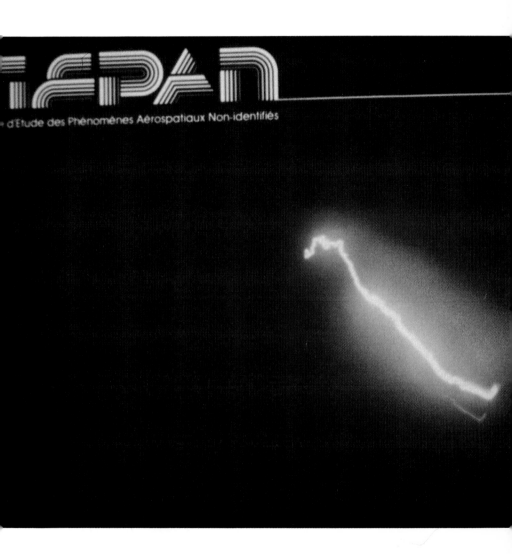

Cover of a booklet outlining the official functions of GEPAN.

IF UFOS ARE REAL
By John Schuessler

Are there living creatures somewhere else in the universe? Many of our best scientists think so. People who are not scientists think so, too. In a 1987 Gallup Poll, 50% of the American people believed that "people somewhat like ourselves are living on other planets in the universe."

Our sun is a star. It has nine planets. It is just one of more than 300 billion stars in our Milky Way galaxy. Astronomers think that about 30 billion of those stars have planets. What if only one planet out of every 100 has developed intelligent life? That would mean there might be 30 million civilizations out there.

Since our sun is a young star (by astronomical standards), older and more developed planets may exist. Other societies may have ways of space travel we cannot even dream about.

The NASA Ames Research Center and Stanford University worked together on a study to try to find life in space. The study was called Project Cyclops. They began by gathering all the known facts about life in space. Then they studied all the possible ways of contacting that life. Their study was finished in 1971. Then other scientists began similar studies.

The Cyclops scientists concluded that most stars have planets. Some of those planets would be at the proper distance from their sun so that life could develop. Many of those planets could then be similar to earth.

The evidence is very strong that other stars do have planets, but we do not have absolute proof. A planet around a star causes the star to wobble as it moves through space. After observing these star orbits for many years, scientists finally found one in 1949 that might have a planet. It is near the double star named 61 Cygni. In 1951 the star system Lelande 21185 was found to have a similar partner. By 1963 Barnard's Star, only 6 light years from Earth, was found to have a planet-like companion.

Canadian astronomers believe they have found seven planets around distant stars. They used a new way of watching star motion that is 100 times more sensitive than the method used before.

Clues to life in space can also be found in meteorites. They are stony or metallic rocks that come from outer space. Most of them burn up as they enter the earth's atmosphere. Then we see them as meteors, or shooting stars. When they do not burn up, they hit the earth. Then we find them as meteorites. Scientists have been studying the Murchison meteorite, which was found in Australia about 20 years ago.

We know that certain chemicals are needed for life to exist. Some of them have been found in the Murchison meteorite. This means that the basic chemicals of life were formed in space long ago. It means that we are one step closer to finding life in space.

THE SEARCH FOR LIFE IN SPACE
By John Schuessler

People have talked about the possibility of life in space for many years. But how could they look for it? Should they look through telescopes?

Visual telescopes gather light. They make an image look brighter. A visual telescope with a camera is better yet. The camera film can gather a lot more light than human eyes. The best photos you see of the planets and galaxies have all been taken with very long time exposures. Astronomers no longer study the stars by looking directly through telescopes. They take long time 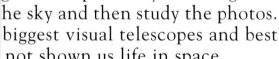 he sky and then study the photos. biggest visual telescopes and best not shown us life in space.

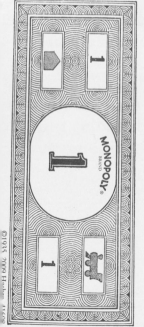 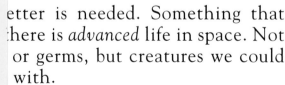 etter is needed. Something that here is *advanced* life in space. Not or germs, but creatures we could with.

Radio telescopes, which gather radio waves may help.

Radio telescopes must be very large. They resemble big mattress springs, spread across a field, or they can look like large satellite "dishes." The radio waves or signals can be recorded by a moving pen writing across a chart. Radio signals from space look like spikey lines moving up and down on a chart.

Radio waves coming from space were discovered in 1931. But they were not a "program" from another civilization. It was found that many natural objects in the sky give off radio waves. The sun, moon, some planets, and even other galaxies give off radio waves. It is easy to tell that these are not signals from other beings because they do not have patterns.

The search for life in space, using radio telescopes, really did not begin until 1960. A scientist named Frank Drake did this early work. It took place at the National Radio Astronomy Observatory in Green Bank, West Virginia. Dr. Drake's first job was to find planets in other solar systems. He aimed a radio telescope, 85-feet across, at two stars. One of those stars, Epsilon Eridani, does seem to have a planet in orbit around it.

Scientists like to give their projects names. Dr. Drake's work was "Project Ozma," named after the *Wizard of Oz*. Other projects to find life in space have been called SETI, which stands for the Search for Extraterrestrial Intelligence. Since Dr. Drake's early work, there have been more than 50 SETI projects. Some of the work was done by Russian scientists.

NASA scientists think the search for life in space should begin by looking at stars that are like our sun. Then, they can look for planets which are like our earth. There are about 800 stars to investigate. NASA will begin this program in 1992. Then they want to search the whole sky. They want to be able to list all the "radio sources" in the sky.

SETI receivers will listen for radio signals from stars as close as 4.5 light years away and as far as 1,000 light years away. The signals will travel at the speed of light, which is 186,000 miles per *second.* That's pretty fast! That means any message from "them" would take 4.5 years to reach Earth. If they said "Hello" and we wanted to answer "Hello to you, too", it would be 9 years from their saying "Hello" before they received our reply. If a planet was 1,000 light years away, the "Hello" – "Hello to you, too" messages would take 2,000 years to complete. You might send the message, but your great, great, great, great grandchildren would still be waiting for the answer.

Some civilizations we hear from may be far more advanced than we are, but none will be less advanced. We don't expect more primitive life forms to be able to communicate with us at all. So, we will be able to learn a lot from anyone who sends a signal to us.

What if we received a message from a civilization 1,000 light years away? It might mean they are 1,000 years more advanced than we are. Now wouldn't *that* be exciting!

Have the SETI scientists ever picked up a signal from space? Yes. The very first day on Project Ozma, Dr. Drake received a 2-minute signal. But it was found to be only interference from a source on Earth. At Ohio State University in 1977, scientists also recorded a short burst of radio energy. The signal was given the name "Wow!" because that was what a scientist said when he saw it recorded on the chart. Another project receives about two "interesting" signals each year, but they never repeat exactly in a mathematical way. That suggests that they could not come from other civilizations out in space.

What will scientists do when a real signal does arrive? First, they will need to be very careful, and make sure that the signal is real. Then they will want to share the information with countries all over the world. Some people think that the United Nations should be asked to speak for planet Earth. At that time we will become citizens of the universe.

Strange Medusa-like cloud near a NATO Base in Uiborg, Jutland, Denmark on the morning of November 17, 1974.

EXOPSYCHOLOGY
By John Schuessler

How do beings from other planets behave? What do they think? What are their personalities like? Do they use body language? How do they communicate? Scientists planning to meet space beings will want to know the answers to these questions. Answers will come from a new branch of science known as *exopsychology*. It means the behavior of beings not from the planet Earth.

Life in space could take many forms. Some forms may be able to speak with us and some may not. If ufologists (people who study UFOs) are correct, some of them may already be visiting Earth. Eventually, we may need to deal with extraterrestrial life forms in one way or another.

The human life span is limited by the aging process, disease, and life style. Extraterrestrial societies may live much longer than humans. What if they live 1,000 years? If so, their needs and desires may be quite different from ours. They may have very strong ethics and morals, or they may have none. They may view humans as lower life forms, and deal with us as we deal with wild animals.

The science and technology of an advanced civilization may seem like magic to us. We may not understand it at all. They may not even be able to explain it to us.

Beings from another planet would find among humans many different ideas, religions, cultures and rules. They would see people of various sizes, shapes and colors. Think of all the languages we speak on Earth. Think of all the other differences Earth people have.

Exopsychologists can help us prepare for the day when we will meet beings from other worlds. They will develop plans for humans to follow when dealing with beings who may be very different from us. This branch of science could even help the people of Earth to better understand ourselves and one another.

Former President Ronald Reagan said "...we often forget how much unites all the members of humanity. Perhaps we need some outside universal threat to make us recognize this common bond. I occasionally think how quickly our differences worldwide would vanish if we were facing an alien threat from outside this world."

Close-up of unexplained lights near Empire State Building in New York City on May 9, 1984.

SPACE TRAVEL IN THE FUTURE
By John Schuessler

Our space program is making good progress. In a little more than 30 years we have moved from being an earth-bound society to a spacefaring one. In the 1950s we were not sure that man could survive in space. Then Project Mercury showed that man could go into space and return safely. Science fiction quickly became science fact. Since then, many other nations have joined us in space.

Many of our space flights have been in the part of space near our planet Earth. A few times we have gone to the moon or sent out space probes. Now, to quote "Captain Kirk" of *Star Trek* we need to "boldly go where no man has gone before." The only way to do this is to develop new space vehicles.

Could such a "Starship" be built using what we know today? In 1978 the British Interplanetary Society studied that question. They decided that a Starship could be built, but some technology improvements are needed. A powerful source of energy is needed to run the electrical and propulsion systems. They thought the power should come from nuclear energy. Life support, guidance and radio systems are already good enough for a Starship.

Since we are always finding new ways to do things, we can make improvements as we go along. When the United States launched the Skylab in 1973, it was the world's first space station. It used both old and new technology. The rocket that launched it, for example, was the same one used for our flights to the moon. The solar telescope, life support system, and many of the experiments were new.

Since that time, the Soviet Union has launched several smaller space stations. They have been very successful. Russian cosmonauts have lived in their "Mir" (which means "peace") space station for as long as a year. They kept adding new modules and new equipment to the Mir.

The new U.S. space station called Freedom is planned for a useful life of 30 years in space. When it becomes active in 1996, it will serve as a base for future space exploration. "Freedom" will grow and change as its systems are improved. In this way, it will never get old.

The rapid growth of computer science is a big help in our space program. Without computers, most of our trips outside the earth's atmosphere could not have happened. Engineers are working on ideas for even better computers and better software. Turning these ideas into reality will not happen until after the year 2000. That means the students in school today will be the ones who will make it all happen.

PREPARING FOR THE FUTURE
By John Schuessler

We live in an era where space travel is becoming common. Each day we learn more about Venus and Neptune and our other planetary neighbors. We have been to the moon and are planning a manned trip to Mars. Scientific breakthroughs happen every day. Still, UFOs remain a mystery.

Perhaps the problem lies in the way we try to solve the UFO mystery. Many people see UFOs, but few report them. And only a few of the reported UFOs ever get investigated. When someone does take the time to examine the report, it may be treated as if it were the only time a UFO has ever been reported. The report may go into a file and the investigator waits for the next one.

Perhaps the biggest problem of all is caused by researchers trying to explain all UFO reports in terms of our present level of technology. If UFOs are from a planet far more advanced than we are, that won't work at all. A limited understanding of technology will not explain a technology that is more advanced. Our 20th Century science cannot tell us the answers. The real answer may lie somewhere in 21st Century science, or even beyond.

Our scientists believe there is life in space that could communicate with us. That is reason enough to build large radio telescopes so that we may listen for messages from space. Of course, any beings able to communicate across the light years of space may have very advanced space programs. Their technology may be quite different from ours. Perhaps we will not recognize it. Perhaps it will appear as magic to us.

It is important to keep an open mind about future science and how it will be used. Thinking like a *futurist* will allow this to happen and it is very easy to do. Futurists are open to all types of new ideas. They constantly search for new information about the world. Exciting new ideas make them very happy. No new idea seems to faze a futurist! They think in global, or even extraterrestrial terms.

Futurists don't believe in words like "impossible" or "it can't be done." They know that many of the things we take for granted today were seen as impossible just a few years ago. So, they use today's science to help think about what tomorrow will be like. They view each new idea as an opportunity to help humanity deal with the future. They use space-age tools like computers, models and statistics in their quest for answers. Because they have a great respect for science and historical fact, futurists are respected in their work. Futurists help make things happen.

UFOs have been a challenge to science for more than 40 years. Perhaps it is time to seek real answers to this mystery once and for all. The futurist outlook may give us the answers and help us advance in space at the same time.